David Livingstone

David Livingstone

Missionary to Africa

AMBASSADOR INTERNATIONAL
Greenville, South Carolina • Belfast, Northern Ireland

David Livingstone:
Missionary to Africa

First printing, 2004
Printed in the United States of America

Cover design & page layout by A & E Media — Paula Shepherd
Cover illustration by Portland Studios — Justin Gerard
Edited by Rebecca Hammond

ISBN 1 932307 24 9

Published by the Ambassador Group

Ambassador Emerald International
427 Wade Hampton Blvd.
Greenville, SC 29609
USA
www. emeraldhouse.com

and

Ambassador Publications Ltd.
Providence House
Ardenlee Street
Belfast BT6 8QJ
Northern Ireland
www. ambassador-productions.com

The colophon is a trademark of Ambassador

Contents

CHAPTER 1

As a Boy

any years ago, the minister of a church in Scotland was very disappointed because only one new member had joined the church in a whole year, but that one was David Livingstone, whose name was later to be known all over the world as a missionary hero and a fearless explorer.

As a boy David lived near the banks of a great river in Scotland called the Clyde. He never had much time for play because he lived in days, happily gone by, when little boys whose fathers and mothers were not rich were sent to work in factories when they were about seven years of age. They worked from early morning until late in the evenings and did not have a holiday, even on Saturdays. David's father and mother were poor people, and they had to put David to work early to help get bread and butter, and boots and clothes, for his little brothers and sisters. But they were very kind parents, and very good, godly people who taught their children to love Jesus and to live as He would like them to live. Still, David's father, though he worked hard selling tea in small packets from door to door, did not find it easy to pay the rent of even a little room in Blantyre and keep his boys and girls clothed and fed.

David's father and mother were Scots whose ancestors had lived in the mountains, and been made strong and healthy by working in the open air and eating plenty of simple food. So David was always thankful for his parentage, and when he grew up he was proud that the Livingstones had always been honest, God-fearing people, who could look anybody in the face without needing to be ashamed. And they were brave people, too! One of David's ancestors had died fighting for his king at the battle of Culloden. David's mother brought up her children in the love and fear of God, and his father set them a good example by being pious and truthful and unselfish.

In those days little boys did not have many books written for them. People did not like their children to read stories; and cheap picture books had not yet been invented. But David read his Bible a good deal, and he was very fond of studying the great "book" of Nature. He loved to roam along the banks of the Clyde, looking for fossils and flowers and butterflies. From this he learned the habit of observing little things that other people did not notice; and that proved of very great value to him when he grew up and traveled in places where other white people had never been. David's father was very fond of books of travel, and he told his boys about the adventures of explorers and missionaries in far off lands, while David's mother told her children stories of Scottish history. So, though the lad had not many books, he learned a great deal from his parents.

When he was ten years old, David left school and went to work in a cotton mill amidst the rattle of machinery. But even though he could no longer attend school, he was determined that he would educate himself to the best of his ability. When his mother gave him his allowance from his first week's wages, he went out and bought a Latin Grammar. When he was tending his loom in the cotton mill, he propped up the book so that he could glance at it for a minute and learn his declensions. Afterwards he bought other books, and read and studied at a night school. Night school finished at ten; then he would go home to supper and read until twelve o'clock or later, until sometimes his mother had to take his books away and send him off to bed. David usually tumbled into bed at nights very, very tired; and when the bell rang for him to get up at five o'clock the next morning, he must have wished that there was more than one Sunday in every week.

In spite of his strict work schedule, David was a fun-loving boy. He liked nothing better than to get a rod and line and go fishing. Once he caught a salmon, which he was not supposed to keep, but he did not think God put fish into rivers for rich people to keep for themselves, so he took it home. He slipped the salmon down one leg of his brother's trousers, and as the boys walked home, the villagers glanced sympathetically at Charlie's swollen leg and thought it must be hurting him very badly.

David was still young when he made Jesus the King of his life, and he did his best to live his life according to God's Word, realizing even as a youth that it was not enough to only talk about his Christianity. Jesus said that He would know His disciples by their fruits. So he set himself to be known as one of Christ's men, not by what he said, but by what he was. His Sunday-school teacher told him to make religion the everyday business of life, not a thing of fits and starts; adding, that if he did that, temptations would not get the better of him.

How David Livingstone came to be a missionary is a rather long story. But it was a letter written by a German missionary named Gutzslaff ministering in China that first set his heart burning to go and tell the heathen about Jesus and His love. Gutzslaff's letter informed the English of how much the Chinese needed Jesus as their Savior, igniting in David a desire to work alongside the missionary. But David also wanted to be able to cure the sick bodies of the Chinese, as a doctor, as well as to lead them to salvation by preaching the Gospel. There were not many medical missionaries at that time, and to be trained as a doctor cost a lot of money. David may have been poor, but he was very determined. He worked hard all through the summer months in the cotton mill, saving every penny he could, so he could go to a medical college at Glasgow all winter. Even then he could not pay all his college fees, and he had to borrow a little money from his brother and pay it back later.

Besides being diligent in his studies, David was clever with his hands. He could use all kinds of tools and do all sorts of odd jobs; and many years afterwards he used to say that being a jack-of-all-trades was a great help to him when he was journeying in Africa far away from blacksmiths and wheelwrights who could mend his wagons. When he had been studying medicine for two years, David went to the London Missionary Society and asked them to send him out to China; but a war was raging in China, and the Society decided to let Livingstone go to Africa instead.

David's interest in Africa was aroused at a meeting at which Dr. Robert Moffat, another famous missionary, spoke of his work in that great continent. Dr. Moffat was then working at Kuruman in Bechuanaland, and he told David after the meeting that from his headquarters there, he could see the smoke of a thousand villages to which no missionary had ever been to take the Gospel story. But before he could be a missionary at all, David had to go to college again—this time at a little town in Essex called Ongar. He worked hard at school and applied himself diligently to his studies.

One day, David wanted to see a relative of his father's who was in London, twenty-four miles away. There was no train or bus, so David walked the whole way. Then, when he had seen his relative, he set out to walk back to Ongar; but on the way he stopped to help a lady who had fallen out of a carriage and hurt herself. Then he missed the road, and walked a long distance off his track; but at last by starlight, he found a signpost that put him on the right road again. It was twelve o'clock at night when he reached Ongar, and he had been walking since three in the morning. He was tired out and white with exhaustion, and somebody had to help him to his bed. He had walked nearly sixty miles in one day! He slept until well into the following afternoon.

CHAPTER 2

To Africa

y the time David was ready to go out to Africa as a missionary, he had grown into a very strong young man. He had coaxing, gleaming hazel-blue eyes like his mother and a slow, steady, swinging gait—as if he could go on walking forever.

In 1840, David sailed from London in a ship called the *George*, and on the way to South Africa the ship called at Rio de Janeiro, South America, making the trip a very long one indeed. But David wasted no time even during the five-month voyage.

He learned from the captain how to use the ship's sextant and how to tell in what latitude and longitude the ship was by observing the sun and the stars.

When he arrived at the Cape, he was detained there for some time, awaiting the necessary papers to continue. He passed the time by going to the Observatory, where Sir Thomas Maclean helped him to study astronomy. This knowledge was of great value to Livingstone when he was making journeys in strange parts of Africa. He had a watch, but he could not have told if it were keeping exact time unless he had been able to check it by the sun; and though his magnetic compass told him where north was, he wanted to know also in what latitude and longitude he was.

Not much was known about Africa when Livingstone went there. The coastline was inhabited here and there by white people; and a few brave people—mostly missionaries—had pushed their way a bit into the interior. Livingstone went first to Kuruman, where the great missionary Robert Moffat worked. David stayed with the Moffat's and helped at their mission for a while and during that time he met and fell in love with Dr. Moffat's daughter Mary.

David did not stay long at Kuruman. His heart's desire was to be a pioneer, to go where other people had never been. There were hundreds of thousands of African natives who had never heard of Jesus Christ, and David journeyed among them fearlessly. He had to live on different food than he was used to in Scotland. One day he ate rhinoceros steak, which he described as "toughness itself."

Wherever he went, he was a shining light for his Lord, doing good for those around him. He befriended a chief whose injured eyes he had healed. One day a little girl of twelve hid under his wagon. She had run away because she was going to be sold as a slave. A man with a gun came to take her away, but the little girl removed her beads and bribed the man to go away. Then David hid her away to keep her safe. "Though fifty men had come for her," he said, "they would not have got her."

When David saved that little African girl from being sold as a slave, he did not know that it would change the whole course of his life. It was his first encounter with the horrifying atrocity of slavery. David found that Africa was cursed by this terrible trade in men and women and children. The natives lived in tribes, which were constantly fighting and taking prisoners. They took the prisoners and loaded them with heavy wooden chains so that they could not run away, and then sold them to slave-traders. When a man is a slave, he belongs to someone else, who can do whatever he likes with him, even kill him if he wants to. The women and children were sold as slaves too. This wicked trade made David furious and he determined that somehow he would find a way to stop it.

Some people look down on others because of the color of their skin. But David loved the people of Africa, and he devoted his life to them. He knew that God created both black and white people, and that He loves them equally. It is man's heart that matters to God, not the tone of his skin.

The tribes of Africa were many and varied. There were the clever Bushmen and the Bakwena or People of the Crocodile who worshipped the crocodile as their god or "Totem." Livingstone spent some time with the Bakwena, curing their sicknesses, teaching them useful things, and learning their language, and they became very fond of him. Then he stayed among the Bakhatlas, the People of the Monkey, and learned their language, too, so that he could teach them about Jesus and the right way to live. After that he made his home at a place called Mabotsa, a name meaning marriage-feast.

One day, some natives came running to Livingstone. A lion had sprung upon their cattle in the daytime and killed several cows. It was unheard of for a lion, which only prowls at night in search of prey and usually sleeps all day in the shade, to come out in the sunlight and attack cattle. The Mabotsa people, who lived in dread of evil spirits, were terrified, and thought the lions were bewitched.

When the lion came again and killed nine sheep in the daytime, Livingstone thought it was time to do something. He took his gun and gave another gun to one of the natives whom he had trained as a teacher, and they set out for the crest of a hill topped with low trees, where they believed the lions were hiding. Soon they came within sight of a lion. It was sitting on a rock, and the native teacher fired. His bullet missed its mark but hit the rock under the lion. The beast didn't even flinch, but merely looked down and bit at the spot where the lead bullet had splintered in the stone. Then it jumped down and dashed through the ring of natives. Two more lions got away without being shot, and the Bakhatlas were nearing panic, because the lions would now be very angry.

But Livingstone was not about to give up. He went after the lions. Rounding the corner at the base of a hill, he saw a large lion perched on a rocky ledge behind a screen of bushes. David took steady aim and fired twice. He hit the lion with both bullets, but the fearsome creature was not killed. It lashed its tale in anger, and Livingstone put another bullet down the gun barrel and was ramming the charge home when he heard a shout. He glanced up as the lion lunged for him. The huge cat caught his shoulder, and man and beast tumbled to the ground. The wounded lion roared and sank its teeth into the top of Livingstone's left arm, and shook him as if he was no more than a rat. Numb with shock, David felt no pain, nor was he even afraid. The native teacher, ten yards away, aimed his rifle. Both barrels misfired. The lion abandoned Livingstone and leapt upon the teacher. A second native tried to run the ferocious beast through with his spear, but the lion sprang onto him and bore him to the ground. But the wounds Livingstone had inflicted on it finally brought the lion down. The men shakily got to their feet. The lion was dead. David's left arm was crushed into splinters, but he and his companions had survived their encounter with the King of Beasts.

He stayed in Kuruman with the Moffats while he recovered from his injuries, and there asked Mary Moffat to be his wife. They were married and then returned to his home in Mabotsa. His wounds healed but his arm never regained its former strength and the skin displayed eleven tooth marks that he would carry to the end of his life.

The day David and Mary's first child arrived was a day of great joy for the new parents. The Bakhatla people, however, had never seen a white baby before, and observed the infant with perplexity and amusement. David and Mary christened their son Robert, and as the Bakhatla call a mother by her first boy's name, they called Mary "Ma-Robert"—the mother of Robert.

The English were not the only colonists trying to tame the wild beauty of Africa. Dutch colonists settling in South Africa were known as Boers and often fought with both the British and the natives. Livingstone did not think badly of all Boers—indeed, he praised them generally as sober and industrious people. But near Mabotsa lived some Boers who had moved up from Cape Colony and they were very unkind and harsh to the natives. They raided the tribes and stole their cattle and forced prisoners into slavery. They also stirred up other tribes against each other. A Bakhatla chief, Sechele, was a good friend of Livingstone's and greatly feared the Boers, who had been encouraging other tribes to attack his people. His tribe lived in terror of being raided and robbed and made slaves. David stood by his friend and did not hide his dislike of those Boers who robbed the natives and took part in the slave trade. His staunch stand against slavery and his strongly vocalized opinions earned him the hatred of many Boers, and one night, in retaliation of his views, they attacked Livingstone's house and destroyed everything in it.

Sometimes it seems as if the more good a man tries to do, the more enemies he makes, but that only makes good men more determined and drives them on to do even greater things.

Many other adventures came David's way. When he removed from Mabotsa to another village named Chonuane he was driven out by a long drought. No rain fell, and the sun was so hot that all the water dried up. So Livingstone had to move to another place, near a river called Kolobeng. That was the last house he lived in. Afterwards Livingstone had no home. Lions did not worry them there; but there were wild beasts all around the village. From his own doorstep Livingstone shot a rhinoceros that had attacked a hunter's wagon and nearly killed the driver. Though he had to walk ten miles through a forest full of prowling beasts of prey,

Livingstone started off at once to try to heal the man. But when he reached the spot the poor man was dead, so David's journey was wasted. He used to say that "the great God had an only Son and he was sent to earth as a Missionary-Physician," and he wanted to follow in the wake of Jesus, and go about doing good. He was never afraid of anything, because Jesus had promised to be "with you to the end," and he said Jesus was a Gentleman of the highest honor, who would keep his word!

Everywhere he went Livingstone kept his eyes wide open. Nothing escaped his notice. He learned this habit when he went on walks along the Clyde as a boy in Scotland; and in South Africa he found thousands of things to interest him. The humming birds, ostriches, antelopes, fossils, flowers, herbs, trees—all these he studied and collected specimens to send to friends in England. Then he learned to do any number of things for himself. He built houses, made gardens, cobbled boots, doctored sick people, tinkered pots and pans, did carpentry, mended guns, farriered horses, repaired wagons, preached, taught, and lectured. He was his own doctor when he fell ill, as he often did, with fever. He mixed his own medicine. He must often have been very lonely when he went off on his journeys, leaving Mrs. Livingstone and his children behind him. One little baby died, and then he sent his family to England, because Africa was not healthy for them. To his little girl Agnes, he wrote a lovely letter, saying good-bye. "I shall not see you again for a long time, and I am very sorry. I have no nanny now. I have given you back to Jesus, your friend, your Papa who is in heaven. He is always near you...and if you do or say a naughty thing, ask Him to pardon you, and bless you, and make you one of his children. Love Jesus much, for He loves you, and he came and died for you."

CHAPTER 3

Exploring

ear Livingstone's home was the great Kalahari, a desert that stretched so far to the north that people thought that all the inside of Africa was a desert. David wanted to find out if this was true. He made up his mind to cross the desert. The chief Sechele told him no white man could ever cross it; but David said he would try.

He started out in a wagon drawn by oxen and soon was in the midst of the desert, the sand so soft that the wheels of the wagon sank in it. There were plenty of wild animals—antelopes, jackals, hyenas and lions—but there was no water. No wells or rivers or springs—nothing but a sea of white sand.

David had learned from the clever bushwomen, however, that water could be found deep beneath the sand. They dug deep holes, put grass at the bottom, and stuck a hollow stick in the hole. Then they filled it up with sand and sucked the water up the stick. They stored the water in ostrich-egg shells, which are as big as a boy's head, and buried the shells in the sand to keep the water cool.

The trek across the desert was long and hard. The sun scorched his skin and blinded his eyes as it journeyed across the sky. Sometimes the sun and the heat and the need for water made him see things that weren't really there. One day he saw a lake, with waves rippling in the sunlight and trees casting soft shadows. He hurried to the water, but as he came nearer it seemed to draw farther away. Then he realized that the sun's rays dancing on the white sand were causing a mirage. There was a lake three hundred miles to the north, but it was many days before Livingstone found it. He first stumbled across a great river and then discovered the lake, 'Ngami. It was a breathtakingly beautiful place but David could not stay there long because of a dangerous stinging fly called the tsetse. When any one was stung by a tsetse, he feels very drowsy, falls asleep and after a time dies of a fever called sleeping sickness.

It was a great change for Livingstone to paddle in a native canoe down the river he had found, after all the hardships of traveling in a wagon. He had tried riding on an ox, but its skin was loose, and he slipped about on it just as if he were on a saddle that was not buckled on firmly. And the ox had long horns that it dug into David when it tried to spear a fly that was biting it.

The discoveries of the river and the lake proved of course that there was more to the heart of Africa than desert. David greatly desired to reach the natives of Central Africa with the Gospel, and felt that if he could discover a better way to reach their lands than his long journey from the Cape, he might be able to open the way up for other missionaries to follow. He hoped to find a way in from either the west or east coasts, instead of from the south. And his heart glowed with the hope that if he opened a path into the heart of this unknown country, he might stop the slave trade, which he called the open sore of the world.

It was to open up such a path that David began his expedition from Cape Town to Loanda on the West Coast and later that great journey right across Africa to the East Coast. When all his preparations were complete, David set off for the West Coast traveling by ox wagon again. At the end of three months, David was very relieved when Kuruman came into sight and the first stage of his journey was safely completed. From Kuruman he went on into the country of the Makololo whose young chief Sekeletu gave Livingstone a great welcome.

For six months David made Linyanti, the Makololo capital, his headquarters before proceeding with his journey. There the natives gathered around him while he told them the stories of Jesus. They listened eagerly for they soon realized that David not only talked about

Jesus and how He went about teaching the people and healing the sick, but was in these ways so like his Master that, through the way he lived, many of them came to love Jesus too.

David was counting on Sekeletu to help him plan the long journey to Loanda, and when the time came for a start to be made the chief called as assembly of his people over which he presided. Of course there were some who prophesied that the expedition would fail and tried to discourage the rest from having anything to do with it. But Sekeletu was keenly interested in David's plan because he knew that if he succeeded there was a good chance of trade and prosperity coming to his people. When the assembly ended twenty seven of the strongest men of the Makololo were chosen to go with David to the West Coast, not as paid servants, but as companions who were as interested in the success of the expedition as David himself.

Everything needed for the expedition had to be carried on men's heads in small packages, because the journey took them through closely-grown forests, forcing them to travel in single file, across rivers, and over hills, so each man could carry only a little weight, especially as the sun poured its heat fiercely upon them. Many of the men were needed to carry the food, as well as the cooking utensils and blankets. Though it was hot during the day, it was often very cold at night.

In the evenings, when they stopped for the night, David recorded their progress in his journal and noted what he had seen. He made astronomical observations as well, and he made them so carefully and wrote them so exactly, that a great geographer, named Sir Harry Johnston, later said that Livingstone's actual routes in South Central Africa could be exactly traced now from his writings. In all his descriptions of the things he saw, Livingstone was always very exact, and when you have read his word-picture of an African scene, you can almost imagine that it is there in front of you.

There were times on this journey when they had run through all the food that they had brought with them. They suffered greatly from hunger and were glad even to be able to make an occasional meal of the mice and moles that they caught on their way.

Once, as they were crossing a flooded river, David narrowly escaped being drowned. Whenever they came to a river the oxen were loaded with the baggage and were sent into the water to swim across while the men crossed by clinging on to the tails of the oxen. On this occasion however, before David had got hold of this unusual form of towrope, his ox hurried after his companions leaving David in the middle of the flooded river. So greatly was David loved by his natives that immediately when they saw what had happened about twenty of them dived into the water to rescue him, but David had always been a powerful swimmer and he managed, despite the fast flowing currents, to reach the opposite bank safely. The natives, who did not know until then that he could swim almost as well as they could, were delighted at this demonstration that he could "carry himself across a river."

They were passing through the country of the Chiboques when one day their encampment was completely surrounded by Njambe the chief and a dangerous looking band of warriors who waved their swords in the air and seemed to be planning an immediate attack. David's companions grasped their spears and prepared to stand their ground when the attack came, but David, anxious as always to avoid any bloodshed, calmly unfolded his campstool and sat down. Then he asked the chief to come forward and sit opposite him that they might have a parley. Njambe with some of his counselors came forward, but his warriors also closed in and threatened David and his friends with their weapons. David realized he was in very great danger but he knew that God was with him. Quietly he told Njambe that all he wanted was to be allowed to pass through his country in peace. At first Njambe refused this request altogether, but David told him that he would not strike first and that if there was a battle the responsibility for it would rest with Njambe. At last when the chief had received presents of beads and clothing, the parley ended happily and David was allowed to carry on his journey without a single shot having been fired.

Many were the hardships suffered by David and his men, arising chiefly from the lack of proper food and the nature of the country through which they were passing. There were times when David was so sick with fever that he could not go on, but had to wait until the fever had left him.

The best of men will sometimes lose heart. David never did because he believed unwaveringly that God had sent him to Africa to open up that great continent and until his work was done he believed that he would be given the strength to carry on. However, some of the Makololo who were with him began to doubt whether they would ever reach the seacoast. They began to fear that their journey was in vain. They grumbled amongst themselves and when David took no notice of their complaints, they staged an open mutiny and declared their intention of returning home to Linyanti. David had already had ample proof of their courage, and he knew that it was not fear of hardship that had caused this trouble so he did not reproach them but tried with kind words to show them that the end of their journey was now in sight, and that if they would have faith a little longer they would shortly be able to laugh at the idea that they had thought of going home when success was so near at hand. They listened in silence so David quietly told them that he himself intended to go on even if he had to travel alone. He entered his tent and knelt down and prayed to God to help him to be brave that he might finish the work that God had given him to do.

David's determination to go on alone had made a great impression upon the Makololo and very soon they felt ashamed that they had proved unfaithful. When David rose from his knees he found the "mutineers" waiting to speak with him. They asked for forgiveness and promised that they would never leave him but would follow him faithfully to the end of the journey. Joy and relief flooded his soul at these welcome words.

At last they reached Cassange where some friendly Portuguese who lived there made them all very welcome, and after a well-earned rest they said good-bye and set off on the last few hundred miles to the coast. At the first sight of the sea stretching out before them to the sky, amazement overwhelmed the Makololo. In wonder, they asked David if they had come to the end of the world.

The long journey together with the many attacks of fever that Livingstone had suffered made it essential for him to take a long rest in Loanda. Mr. Gabriel, a Commissioner appointed by the British Government for putting an end to the slave trade, took David into his home and promptly put him to bed. How glad he was to be in a comfortable bed again after nearly a year sleeping on the ground.

It was four months before David was well enough to set out again. During that time his Makololo natives waited for him to get better without complaining and set to work to earn their living. They hit on the idea of collecting firewood and selling it in bundles to the people of Loanda. It was hard work. They had to go long distances to collect the wood and then carry it to Loanda on their backs.

There were three British cruisers at Loanda patrolling the seas to keep a watch on any ships that might be trying to run a cargo of slaves. One day a coal ship arrived to bring supplies to the cruisers, and Mr. Gabriel arranged that David's Makololo natives should be given a chance to earn some money by unloading the coal ship on to the cruisers. How excited they were to see the cruisers at close quarters! They were like huge floating villages made of iron.

David was offered a passage home to England on one of those cruisers. It was a tempting invitation—no more hunger, no more sleeping on the hard ground, and best of all no more fever. But David chose to stay at Loanda, determined that as soon as he was better he would return to Linyanti with the Makololo natives whom Sekeletu had allowed to come with him. They were prepared to do any kind of work while they waited for their "father" as they fondly called David, and if he went back to England now, even though his health was poor, he felt that he would be deserting them. In addition, he was eager to reach Linyanti again to prepare for the next great journey he was already planning—to find a path to the east coast.

He did send home his journal of observations, along with some maps he had drawn, but the steamer was wrecked on its voyage to England. It took Livingstone some months to rewrite his journal and redraw the maps, but he did it without complaint.

Over one of his discoveries he had a disappointment. He had come to the conclusion that the center of Africa (which people had thought was a desert) was like a great saucer with hills all around it making the rim. And he satisfied himself that there had once been a great lake there. Also he was convinced that this country would be very fertile, and would grow coffee and cotton and vegetable oil pods. Another traveler, Sir Roderick Murchison, had, however, come to the same conclusion before Livingstone, and without Livingstone knowing of it. So the credit of a very important geographical discovery went to someone else.

The journey back took them an entire year. Great was the excitement of the Makololo when, after nearly two years away from home, they came in sight of Linyanti. Dressing themselves in the fine materials they had bought in Loanda with the money that they had earned, they fell into line as they had seen the soldiers do in their drill at Loanda with their guns over their shoulders;

what a welcome they received as they marched along and how glad Sekeletu was to see David again. While they were all excited about their safe return, David called them to a service to give thanks to God who had looked after them and brought them back safely through so many dangers on the journey.

David spent seven weeks in Linyanti making plans for a new expedition to the East Coast and once again he was counting on Sekeletu to provide him with men to go with him. This time when Sekeletu called an assembly of his people together and explained David's plans, hardly had he finished speaking before more than a hundred had volunteered to go with him. The twenty-seven who had made the journey to Loanda were so full of praise for their "father" and had told so many stories of their adventures that even David was surprised at the number who volunteered.

Sekeletu and two hundred of his followers decided to accompany David as far as Kalai. The whole company was fed at the chief's expense from cattle, which he commanded his followers to take with them. Among the baggage were all sorts of things that Sekeletu had provided for the use of David and his men during the journey, including beads and cloth that could be used to buy the favor of war-like tribes or to purchase a canoe or supplies of meal. Nor did David forget to include a supply of flour so that he could bake his own bread—something he had very much missed on his last journey—in a homemade oven.

On the second night, when some of the men had gone on ahead with the supplies, which included a change of clothes for David, there was a terrific thunderstorm that not only drenched the party but completely soaked the ground on which they intended to pass the night. David did not look forward to that prospect one little bit, and he was greatly moved by the kindness of Sekeletu who offered him his own dry blanket, telling David that he was used to sleeping rough whether it was wet or fine and, without waiting to see what David would say about his generous offer, he lay down and rested on the cold, wet ground until morning.

Only a very brave man would have attempted such a great and perilous journey across the African continent; only a very strong man, moved by a holy purpose, could have succeeded. No one had ever done it before. There was no road, not even a track. The people he passed through were cruel and savage. The heat was terrible, and fever made David very weak. He could not preach to the people without knowing their language, but he had a special lantern with which he could show them slides of Bible stories. Although they liked the pictures, the poor, ignorant people, full of fears, were afraid lest the figures in the pictures should enter their bodies as evil spirits. On one occasion some people from a savage tribe stopped

Livingstone from crossing a river, but he took out his watch and let them listen to its ticking. Then he let the sun's rays pass through a small magnifying glass that he had in his pocket, and it acted as a burning glass and caused fire to burn. The natives were so amazed at these wonders that they let David cross in their canoe to the other side of the river.

CHAPTER 4

Across Africa

ivingstone's discovery of a way to the East Coast was one of his greatest feats. During his journey to the West Coast he had won the hearts of the Makololo natives, who had traveled with him. Every man who had set out with him had returned. Not a single life had been lost on that journey, though they had endured many dangers from man and nature and beast. Livingstone proved to the people of Africa what a Christian truly was, treating all men equally no matter their appearance or age or skin color.

David credited much of his influence with the good name the Bakwena people had given him. "No one," he said, "ever gains much influence in this country without purity and uprightness." Livingstone could not afford to pay his people much for their service, but the love he inspired made them loyal and true.

When Sekeletu said good-bye to David at Kalai, the expedition now consisted of 115 people, David and 114 of the Makololo, many of whom were to carry the baggage all the way to the coast.

It was during this journey across Africa that Livingstone had the joy of making a tremendous discovery. He heard from some of the natives about a "smoke that sounds." This was the native's way of describing the mist thrown up by a great waterfall. Livingstone at last came to the spot, and his were the first eyes of a white man to gaze on the marvels of the Zambezi River Falls. Livingstone, who had seen so many great sights, said it was the most wonderful sight he had witnessed in Africa. A mighty river over a mile wide rushed along till it reached a chasm, over which it fell nearly 400 feet. Below the fall the river channel is narrow, and the wide stream is squeezed into about a hundred yards. Columns of fine misty spray, two or three thousand feet high, leap into the air, and are blown about by the breeze. From an islet at the top of the falls Livingstone watched this majestic spectacle. Then he planted coffee beans as well as apricot and peach stones by the edge of the falls, hoping that trees would grow. Livingstone gave the falls the name "Victoria Falls," in honor of Queen Victoria, and he carved "D.L., 1855"—his initials and the year of his discovery—on a tree growing nearby. For a moment, he felt guilty of vanity; but then he excused it, as it was the only instance when he had been vain.

A very tender heard beat in David Livingstone's breast. On one of his great journeys he had among his companions a poodle that he called Chitane. Livingstone was very fond of this faithful dog, which he said had more pluck than a hundred country dogs. Chitane took charge of the whole line of march during the journeys. He would run to see the first of the line of bearers, back to the last, barking as if urging them on. When the line stopped, Chitane would find out which hut Livingstone occupied, and would not let a country cur come in sight of it. He never stole anyone's food, and did not let other dogs steal either. In crossing a marsh a mile wide and waist deep, Chitane came to a sad end. "I went over first," David later wrote, "and forgot to give directions about the dog, and all were too much engaged in keeping their balance to notice that he swam among them until he died." Livingstone grieved over poor Chitane's death, but refused to let his sorrow keep him heavy hearted. He was always ready to be cheerful if there was but the smallest warrant for it. At the time, he was ill from his diet of maize, millet porridge, and mushrooms, but he brightly said, "we got a cow yesterday, and I am to get milk tomorrow."

Generally when Livingstone was going through a strange land he asked leave from the tribe who owned it to pass through their country, explaining that he was on a peaceful errand. Once or twice suspicious tribes would bar the way. On one occasion when he asked for leave to cross the Zambezi River, a howling mob barred the way and a native rushed out with an axe to stop Livingstone, who thought he was going to have his head chopped off by a mad savage, and felt that would be a sorry way to leave the world. Then one of the natives asked David who he was.

"I am an Englishman!" he answered.

"Ah," said the natives, who lived near a Portuguese settlement, "you must be one of that tribe that loves the black man." They then moved out of the way and allowed Livingstone to pass.

Soon after that the journey was ended at a place called Quilimane, where he saw the sea, and knew that he had opened a new way into Central Africa.

CHAPTER 5

By River and Lake

After crossing Africa, a tremendous feat, Livingstone, who had been fifteen years without a holiday, came home to England. He was grieved to find his father dead; but he was glad to see his wife and his children again. All England was proud of him. Queen Victoria sent for him to hear his story from his own lips, and all kinds of great people went to listen to his lectures. He was given a gold medal by the Royal Geographical Society, and the book that he wrote was read by every one who could buy or borrow a copy. The Directors of the London Missionary Society made a hero of David, and when he asked for more missionaries to go out to the heart of Africa, they promised to send them.

Soon Livingstone, though he loved being in England, yearned to be back in Africa. The Dark Continent called

him, and the welfare of the African people was on his
heart. He wanted to go back to make an open path for
Christianity and commerce.

This time David did not go out from the London
Missionary Society, but as a servant of the British
Government. David was no less a missionary, but he was
a pioneer, opening up new roads and exploring lands and
discovering peoples never before visited by white men.
Thus it was as a pioneer and as an explorer that David
returned, for much as he would have loved to continue
working under the London Missionary Society, they did
not have the money to arrange this journey, and David
was certain that this and other such journeys must be
made if the way was to be opened up for the Gospel to
reach the people in the heart of Africa.

Lord Palmerston, who was then Prime Minister, and
Lord Clarendon, the head of the Foreign Office, provided
David with money and equipment for a journey into the
valley of the River Zambezi. This was the first journey
where other white men went with him including Dr.
Kirk who wanted to study the plant life in Africa. His
brother Charles Livingstone accompanied David to act
as his secretary and help him write up his reports on all
that they saw on their journey. Captain Bedingfield came
as skipper of the small steamer, which was to be taken
out in pieces and fitted together before being launched
on the River Shire. This steamer, specially made for the

navigation of the River Zambezi, was named the *Ma-Robert*, Mrs. Livingstone's African name.

Alas, the *Ma-Robert* was a great disappointment. Everything that could go wrong with a ship seemed to go wrong. First its boiler-fire ate up too much fuel, and then its engines were noisy and did not work smoothly. The steamer wheezed like a person with a bad cold in his chest, so Livingstone called it "The Asthmatic."

When the party reached the mouth of the Zambezi the *Ma-Robert* was fixed together and in it they set sail to examine the various inlets of the river. The Portuguese had always said that only one of these inlets could be used for ships and all the maps that were printed only marked the Kilimane as navigable, but David soon discovered that the maps were wrong.

There were four inlets to the river apart from the Kilimane and all of them were suitable for shipping. David realized that the Portuguese had printed those maps all wrong for a wicked purpose of their own. They wanted to keep the British cruisers watching the Kilimane while they used the other routes for collecting cargoes of slaves without interference. By discovering their insidious plan, David was able to have true maps sent home to the British Government and strike one more blow in the fight to stop slavery.

Steaming up the Kangare, one of the tributaries of the Zambezi, they made slow progress as far as Tete where David had left his Makololo to wait for his return from England. Great was their joy when they recognized him, though at first they were afraid to touch him lest they should spoil his new clothes. What a lot they had to tell him of their adventures while he had been away. They had been treated very kindly by Major Sicard of the Portuguese garrison who had given them land to grow their own food, but they had faced real hardships too. Six had been killed by Bonga, a hostile native chief, and thirty had died of smallpox.

It was impossible, owing to the rapids that extended for more than eight miles along the river, to make progress in the Ma-Robert, so from Tete a report to the British Government was sent asking for a more suitable ship to be sent out. Meanwhile, leaving the *Ma-Robert* at Tete, the party set off overland in the direction of an inland lake that they decided to explore. This turned out to be Lake Shirwa—a great sheet of water surrounded by swamp.

At one native village ruled by a chief called Tingane, about 500 armed men blocked the path of Livingstone and his party. It looked a very dangerous situation, but Livingstone boldly went forward and asked to meet the headmen of the tribe. He explained that they had come in peace and only wanted to explore the lands beyond. Tingane at first was afraid that David and his party had come hunting for slaves and that explained this show of force. Until David and his party reached Lake Shirwa, the only white men they had seen had no love for the Africans and had only come in search of slaves to sell in Europe. Many were the brave battles that Tingane and his people had fought to keep their liberty. When he knew why David had come and heard how he was set against the slave trade, he was most friendly and called his people together. The chief explained to his people that they had nothing to fear from these men who only wanted to help the people of Africa.

They returned to the river and embarked once more in the *Ma-Robert*. They slowly progressed about 200 miles until they reached a number of cataracts that they named "The Murchison" after Sir Roderick Murchison who had proved a great friend to the expedition. The crocodiles surprised by this invasion of their kingdom several times rushed towards the ship as if they intended an attack, but having at close quarters gained some idea of its size they must have thought better of it and retreated.

Supplies being now exhausted, they made their way down river again to the Kangare where they were able to obtain fresh provisions from one of the British cruisers that was on duty there. The *Ma-Robert* had to be beached this time for repairs, but when the job was completed they set off again towing behind several smaller boats in which supplies and men for which there was no room in the *Ma-Robert* were carried. Unfortunately, one of the Makololo was drowned when one of these boats capsized.

At a place called Mboma they laid in fresh supplies of food and as they were staying the night there, one of the natives decided to entertain them by playing on an instrument with one string, the like of which David had never seen before. After a while the entertainment, which was especially for David's benefit—the musician never having seen a white man before—became rather monotonous and David was glad to put an end to the concert by making a present of a piece of cloth to the musician—the equivalent in Africa of "giving him a penny to go into the next street."

Leaving the *Ma-Robert* in the care of the rest of the party, David set off with three of his English companions and thirty-six Makololo to search for Lake Nyassa. Many were the strange people they met on the way; they were generally friendly when David had explained his object at a palaver, and often willing to help him with such supplies as he required for the journey.

Of all the strange ornaments which the natives are accustomed to wear, the strangest that David saw were the Pelele worn by Mansanja women. The upper lip is pierced and the hole is gradually widened until there is a gap of about two inches; into this an ivory ring is forced until the lip stretches a couple of inches beyond the end of the nose.

Livingstone and Dr. Kirk were the first Europeans to see Lake Nyassa, one of the three largest African lakes. When they eventually reached the southernmost point there lay before them a lake so tremendous in extent that they had no means of knowing its length. Later they were to discover that it stretched for over 300 miles, about as far as from London to Edinburgh.

David now felt it was time to return to Linyanti to take back the Makololo who had been in his service for so long. Not all of them went with him for some had married in Tete and preferred to settle there, and others had unfortunately taken to the evil ways of some of the half-cast people of Tete who were heavy drinkers. Leaving the *Ma-Robert* in the care of ten English sailors in Tete, David set out with Dr. Kirk, his brother and the remainder of the Makololo.

Progress was slow, partly due to the terrific heat of the sun, which made the earth and the rocks almost unbearable to the bare feet of the natives. David managed to keep them on the march for about six hours each day, walking about two miles an hour, but even then the natives complained of being tired. Living in Tete had spoiled them for the more energetic kind of life that they had always been used to when Livingstone first traveled with them from Linyanti.

On one occasion the natives were grumbling that the journey was too long, and David saw that they were getting rebellious and were likely to start stealing his stuff to prevent him from going on. In order to stop them Livingstone dashed out of his shelter waving his pistol and looking as if he meant business. The natives soon listened to him as he warned them that they were not to think that they could take things that did not belong to them. As they became more reasonable, his voice grew less severe, and then he forgave them for their bad conduct.

As they passed through the Chicova plains a chief named Chitóra came out to meet the party to welcome them and make them a present of food and drink. He told them he had heard of Dr. Livingstone and had always wanted to meet him as he knew that he was a friend to the people of Africa. Anything he had was there for David and his party to use. It must have warmed David's heart to know that he was not only opening up new ways into the heart of Africa but was finding a way into the heart of her peoples too.

The journey took them among many strange tribes. The Batokas for example had never seen any white men before and were at first very alarmed by their appearance. They told David that their fathers had never told them about people like him. They said that they had seen stranger things, therefore, than any of their ancestors in seeing him and his two companions. A doubtful compliment but no doubt Livingstone appreciated their friendly interest.

As they approached Linyanti they were sad to hear that a mission that had followed David there several years before had failed. It was not a healthy neighborhood for

Europeans and of the nine who had settled there five had died within a year. The rest, some of whom were sick with fever, had moved to another place.

At Linyanti they received a welcome, but it was nothing like the welcome they had on their return from Loanda. The reason was soon plain. Sekeletu had contracted leprosy and in his illness had forgotten much of David's teaching about the love of God. He now believed that he had been bewitched and that his leprosy was some kind of curse. David was sad to find his old friend so ill and at once went to call on him where he lay away from his own people in a covered wagon. The chief was glad to see David again. A woman witch doctor was attending him when David arrived; he ordered her to leave him that he might try the white man's medicine. David did everything he could for him and not only tried to cure him of his leprosy but also tried to give him back his faith in the Good News of the loving Father who sent His Son into the world to save the African and the Englishman and who made no difference between them.

At Linyanti David discovered that the trustworthy people of Sekeletu had kept all his medical supplies safe. The missionaries who had been working there during David's absence had all the medicines they needed to cure their diseases, of which some of them had died, within a few yards of their camp and never knew it.

Although the Makololo would not have thought of touching David's property while he was away and although they accepted the teaching of the Bible, David found that they were not so careful about stealing cattle from their neighbors. When he told them that this was wrong they could not understand why. Had their neighbors any right to cattle if they could not fight for them? Besides these cattle that they had taken were probably directly descended from the cattle which at one time had belonged to the father of Sekeletu, so could it be stealing to take back what had once been theirs?

When David and his small party set out to return to Kongone, Sekeletu was too ill to go with him but still generously supplied food and oxen for the journey, as well as a number of canoes for traveling down the valley of the Zambezi.

It was as they crossed the Mburuma rapids that once again David had cause to be grateful to his Makololo followers. As they were crossing the rapids two of the canoes filled with water. Jumping out of the canoes they swam alongside until they reached the foot of the rapid and then ran alongshore to begin baling the water out. Had they not done so it is more than likely that everyone in them would have been drowned. It was in moments like this that they proved how much they loved David—even more than their own lives.

It is a pity to think that this great people—the Makololo—were shortly to lose their power and influence as a tribe, but with their chief grievously ill, that is exactly what happened. A few years after Sekeletu died, the great kingdom that he had ruled so wisely since the age of eighteen was broken up and his people scattered to the winds.

BUSHMAN'S CAMP

AMAZON WARRIORS

CHUMA AND SUSI

VICTORIA FALLS

THE GIRAFFE

AFRICAN LION

AFRICAN RIVALS

FARM SCENE IN THE CAPE COUNTRY

THE TRAGEDY OF CENTRAL AFRICA

PREACHING ON THE JOURNEY UP-COUNTRY

"I READ THE BIBLE THROUGH FOUR TIMES
WHILE I WAS IN MANYUEMA."

THE MANYUEMA ABUSHCADE

STANLEY FINDS LIVINGSTONE

LION ENCOUNTER

LIVINGSTONE ATTACKED BY LION

NIGHT IN THE WILDERNESS

DANGEROUS HIPPOPOTAMI

MIDNIGHT CONFLICT WITH A LEOPARD

HUNGRY VISITORS

CUNNINGLY HUNTING OSTRICH

FISHING SCENE IN ANGOLA

COMPULSORY SERVICE IN ANGOLA

A VILLAGE OF ANGOLA

BURIAL PLACE

SCENE ON THE LEEAMBYE

GRAVE OF MRS. LIVINGSTONE

CHITAPANGWA RECEIVING DR. LIVINGSTONE

RHINOCEROS HUNT

THE PIT

MISSION STATION, KOLOBENG

"THE MAIN STREAM CAME UP TO SUSI'S MOUTH."

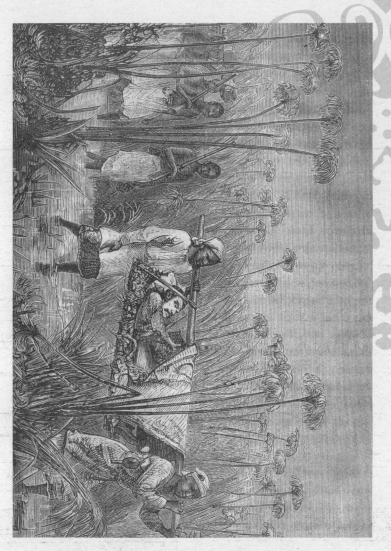

THE LAST MILE OF LIVINGSTONE'S TRAVELS

CHAPTER 6

Freeing Slaves

avid and his party arrived at Tete where they had left the *Ma-Robert,* but the ship now not only wheezed and coughed but refused to keep afloat at all and had to be abandoned. When they reached Kongone they were welcomed at a new Portuguese customs house where they settled while they awaited the arrival of their new ship. It arrived soon after, followed by two British cruisers carrying on board Bishop Mackenzie and the Oxford and Cambridge missions to the Shire and Lake Nyassa, which consisted of six Englishmen and five Africans from the Cape. They were hoping that David would be able to take them to the Shire but as he was planning an expedition to Rovuma they decided to go with him to see if they could reach Lake Nyassa and the Shire that way. David's new ship, the *Pioneer*, proved a much better craft than her predecessor; however, they ran into shallow water and were forced to return to the sea. They sailed along the coast until they reached the mouth of the Zambezi, and then progressed up the river until the Shire. From there they sailed as far as Chibisa's village.

At Chibisa's they heard that war had broken out in the Manganja country and that a party of slaves would shortly pass through the village on the way to Tete. David, who hated the very idea of slavery, consulted his friends and Bishop Mackenzie and his party, and they decided to do all that they could to free the slaves.

Soon a long line of men, women and children, eighty-four in all, appeared manacled together. Sadly they marched, driven along by African drivers armed with muskets. When they caught sight of David and his party, the drivers with one exception fled into the forest. The one who remained said that he had bought the slaves and that they were his property, but the slaves said that they had been captured in war. Seeing that David was more ready to believe the slaves than himself, he too ran off after the other drivers into the forest.

The captives knelt down and expressed their thanks for this unexpected delivery. They had feared that they were doomed to spend the rest of their lives in slavery. David and his companions cut the ropes that bound the women and children, but it was more difficult to release the men as each man had his neck in a forked stick six or seven feet long and kept in place by an iron rod riveted at both sides across his throat. Fortunatcly the Bishop had a hacksaw in his luggage and one by one the men were freed. David took up the wooden yokes and broke them into pieces on the ground.

When they were all freed, David helped them build fires and prepare a meal. A short while before the natives had been bowed down with sadness; now they began to laugh and smile again as the broken yokes were used to make the fire blaze.

Many of these people were little children of four and under. One little boy said to David, "The others tied us up and starved us; you cut the ropes and tell us to eat. What sort of people are you?" How surprised he and the others would have been if they had known that these men who had set them free had a Master, too, who said, "Take my yoke upon you," especially if they had understood that His yoke would bring them not pain, sadness and despair, but love, joy and peace.

When David told the freed slaves that they might go where they pleased or remain with the party, they all chose to stay with their new friends and in the next few days they were to see many more slaves freed as they had been. One of them named Chuma became so fond of David that he became inseparable from him and went with him on all his journeys.

The bishop and his missionaries settled in among the Manganja people at Magomero. It was a hard time for them to begin their work for while the Manganja were friendly, they were at war with the Ajawa who were responsible for making slaves of all those whom they captured in battle. It was natural that Bishop Mackenzie and his workers, who hated slavery as much as David did, would have wanted to follow the Ajawa, drive them out of the Manganja country and free any slaves they found on the way. David knowing these tribes a lot better advised them not to do so, not because he was afraid of the Ajawa, but because he knew that if he became involved in a tribal war there would be real danger to the mission and all its workers.

When David left the mission settlement that they built at Magomero to set off for Lake Nyassa, they were full of hope about the future of their work among the Manganja. All went well for a time until one day two of the missionaries together with a number of Manganja natives set out to find a quicker route to the Shire. Unfortunately they lost their way and found themselves in a slave-trading village. Knowing that their lives were in danger they prepared to go back the way they had come but the hostile inhabitants seized two of the Manganjas and the rest barely escaped with their lives.

Back at Magomero they related what had happened, and the wives of the two Manganja men who had been taken as slaves persuaded Bishop Mackenzie that he ought to go to their rescue. It was difficult to decide what was best to do, but in the end he decided to attack the village. While David would have been in favor of seeking a peaceful means to free the men who had become slaves, he was saddened later when he heard that the village had also been burned as a punishment, feeling certain that his Master would not have approved, and knowing too, that such an action was going to make it harder for the missionary in Africa whose job it was to preach the Gospel of Love. The end of this mission came soon afterwards. Bishop Mackenzie and several of his companions died, stricken with fever. Bishop Tozer, who followed on to take Mackenzie's place, decided to move the mission from Magomero to Zanzibar, an island base away from the unrest between the tribes, but sadly also away from the Manganja people, who badly needed help at this time when their country was being overrun by slave traders.

For many years, Mrs. Livingstone had been away in Scotland looking after their children, but her heart was always in Africa with her husband and his work. While David was resting between two of his great journeys, she at last was able to rejoin her husband. In spite of the time spent apart, the two grew ever closer and came to love each other more and more with each passing day. They had little time though, before tragedy shattered their happiness. Mrs. Livingstone was stricken with fever. The doctors did all they could to spare her life, but it was not to be. Just a few short months after her return to the land of her birth, she died. David was heartbroken by her death. The man who had faced so many deaths himself and braved so many dangers without fear, broke down and wept like a child. How lonely he felt with his children far away in England, as he buried his beloved Ma-Robert beneath a baobab tree at Shupanga. But he found courage in his Lord to keep a stiff upper lip and carry on his work. "I am determined," he said, "that I will not swerve a hair's breadth from my course."

CHAPTER 7

Across the Ocean

avid had asked for a new vessel especially invented for river navigation to be sent out. This was built in such a way that it could be broken down into pieces quite easily. Each piece was of a size that one man could carry on land, because there would be long stretches of the rivers and lakes which were not navigable, either because they were too shallow or because too much weed grew in the waters. When this new vessel called the *Lady Nyassa* was put together at Shupanga a large crowd of natives assembled to watch. Great was their surprise when this vessel of iron was successfully launched and a great cheer went up as she slipped easily and smoothly into the water.

The *Lady Nyassa*, which had cost £6,000, was paid for by David himself from the money he had obtained from the sale of his book *Missionary Travels,* written when he was last home in England.

Unfortunately about this time, both Charles Livingstone and Dr. Kirk became ill with fever and it became clear that they would have to go home to England. Extremely disappointed because he could not go on with the expedition, David returned with his friends to the coast. He was sad, too, because the British Government thought his mission had not been a success, and stopped sending any more money to pay for his travels. This led to the decision that he must return to England. He would be forced to sell his brand new vessel, but fearing that if he sold the ship in Africa, she would fall into the hands of the slave-traders and be used for the traffic in human beings that he hated so much, he actually crossed the Indian Ocean from Africa to India in his little lake steamer *Lady Nyassa.* After braving all the dangers in Central Africa, David thought little of facing the perils of the ocean in a little cockleshell of a steamer.

The journey to Bombay was nearly two thousand five hundred miles and David navigated the ship all the way by himself, achieving a fine feat of seamanship in a vessel invented, not for the ocean, but for the lakes and rivers of Africa. The white men on board were too ill with fever to help with the running of the ship, so on top of his other responsibilities David had to instruct the crew of natives from the Zambezi country as well.

Livingstone had been looking forward to a long rest and for an opportunity to see his own family from which he had been separated for so many years, but it was not to be. The reports that he had sent home about Lake Nyassa and reports from other explorers about Lake Tanganyika had aroused the wide interest of many in England. Not long after his arrival in Britain, he was visited by Sir Roderick Murchison who persuaded David to prepare for yet another expedition.

Reassuring David that he would look after his family while he was away, Sir Roderick helped him to make all the necessary preparations. Lord John Russell, thinking that David would be expecting some personal reward for all his labors, sent an ambassador to see him to see what honor could be conferred on him, but David, reassured by Sir Roderick's promise that his family would not be in want, would not ask for anything at all for himself, but added "If you stop the Portuguese slave trade you will gratify me beyond measure."

The Government, uncertain about the success of this new expedition, did not provide much money for it and only gave £500. An old college friend of David's gave £1,000 and about £2,000 was raised by public subscription. David gave all the money he earned from his new book written about this time *The Zambezi and its Tributaries*, together with £2,000 that he raised by the sale of the *Lady Nyassa* in Bombay. David provided much himself for the expedition. Unfortunately, after he had gone into the African interior, the bank with which he had deposited his money was ruined and all David's money was lost.

It was fortunate that the Government had appointed David as H.M.'s Consul to the tribes in the interior of Africa, for at least he could depend for some help on the resources of the British Government at a time when his own funds were almost nil.

This journey was destined to be David's last expedition and he was never to see England or his children again. He knew that if Africa was ever to be a Christian land, the slave trade must be stopped and though it might cost him his life he set out to end that trade.

David set off from England, sailed over to France and from there across the seas to Bombay where he had left his two African friends Chuma and Wekorani. Together with them and some Indian natives he sailed for Zanzibar. Soon the party was heading up the Rovuma into the heart of the jungle, which extends along a plateau for many miles between two mountain ranges. Here the trees grew so closely together and the whole area was so completely overgrown with creepers that even in the daytime it seemed dark, but they managed to hack their way through.

It was as they were going through this wild country that some of David's native servants deserted him and refused to take such a perilous journey. To cover up their desertion, they spread a rumor that Dr. Livingstone had been murdered by a party of Mafite at a place called Mapunda. The rumor reached England, but although something of the dangers which David was facing every day was known to the people at home so that no one would have been surprised that David had been violently put to death, there were many of his friends who refused to accept the report until they had heard more details. Among these friends was Sir Roderick Murchison who, along with many others, still hoped for news that would tell them that David was alive.

The first gleam of hope came in a dispatch to the Foreign Office from Mr. Seward who claimed to have spoken to various tribes who had seen David after the date that the rumor said he had died. Sir Roderick Murchison, encouraged by this report, arranged with the Government to cooperate with the Royal Geographical Society in an expedition to Lake Nyassa that would settle the question of whether David was still alive or not. This expedition sailed for Africa and successfully navigated the Zambezi. In a boat built to be carried in sections and assembled on the spot, like Livingstone's *Lady Nyassa*, they crossed the Lake after which that boat was named. They met with Chief Marenga who told them that David was alive and had been in touch with him only a little while before, while some of his men had seen him even more recently still going on further into the interior. Marenga was also able to tell them that he had personally questioned the natives who had deserted David. They had admitted that they did not relish exploring such dangerous places as those in which he was traveling and therefore they had gone home. "There is a limit to all things," they had said. Fortunately for Africa and for the end of the slave trade there, David never recognized any such limits in his expeditions.

Sir Roderick's expedition, although they had not seen David for themselves, returned to the Zambezi and home to England well satisfied that the rumor was groundless and that David was still very much alive.

CHAPTER 8

His Last Major Journey

avid had by now penetrated far into the interior. From the Rovuma he had continued over the watershed above it. Again he reached the shores of Lake Nyassa, seeing many slave-gangs on the way, and even the skeletons and bodies of slaves who had died as they were being hurried to the coast to be sold. It was a terrible journey, through dank forests into which the sunlight could not reach, across dreary swamps, and over rough hills upon which the hot sun beat pitilessly. Deluges of rain swept over David and his men as they toiled along. They had very little food and the hard maize corn broke their teeth. David became so thin that he said anyone could easily guess how much they could get for his bones. A long year's hard journeying brought him to the edge of a lake called Tanganyika. Then he pressed on, and discovered two more great inland seas—Lakes Mweru and Bangweolo—but now David was dangerously ill, and he had to rest to regain his strength.

Often Livingstone's men sorely tried his patience. On this last great journey to Ujiji, Livingstone turned aside to discover Lake Bangweolo, but his men rebelled. They wanted to go straight on to Ujiji. All, excepting five, flatly refused to go with him to the lake. Livingstone did not get angry when his men tried to upset his plans. He felt in his own mind that he could not blame them. They were sick of tramping day by day, carrying their loads. Livingstone was weary of it, too. So when they rebelled he did not scold, but quietly went his way without them. David and his remaining men reached Lake Bangweolo and explored all around it. One day Livingstone waded into the lake, but before long leeches had fastened themselves onto his legs and had to be wrenched off. When he and his men left Bangweolo to return to their journey, the bearers who had refused to go to the lake intercepted them along the path. David's gentleness had touched their hearts, and once again they offered their services to him. Always Livingstone made the utmost allowance for other people's failures and misdeeds. He was conscious of defects in himself, and that made him lenient to others. "I also have my weaknesses," he wrote.

The journey wore on into the beginning of the year 1869. David had contracted an illness that lasted ten weeks and made him so weak he could not walk. A cough worried him by day and robbed him of sleep at night. The bearers carried him in a rude litter, but he was jolted about terribly. Without medicine or food fit for a sick man to eat, Livingstone's plight was grave. Scarcely expecting to get there, he prayed that he might reach Ujiji, where he expected to find medicine and stores, and, above all, letters from home. The hope of those letters stayed with him, but he feared he would not live to read them. Soon he lost count of the days of the week and the month. At last, after enduring agonies, he was rowed across Lake Tanganyika in a canoe to the eastern shore, and landed at Ujiji. But alas, the stores upon whose presence at Ujiji he had counted so confidently were not there. They had been plundered, first on the way from the coast, and then—what remained of them—at Ujiji. Only a few fragments were to be found. The medicine, so sorely needed, had been left behind, thirteen days' journey away. So had the cheese that would have nourished Livingstone in his exhaustion. There was nothing to do but to send to Zanzibar for some more, and sit down to await their arrival at Ujiji. Yet even in this plight David wrote to his daughter, saying that he had broken his teeth tearing at maize, and had "such an awful mouth" that "if you expect a kiss from me you must take it through a speaking trumpet."

CHAPTER 9

Stanley

or two years no news of David had reached the outside world. People were uneasy. They thought he must be dead. At this time the New York Herald sent out a newspaper reporter. The story that the paper wanted was "Where is Livingstone?" Mr. Stanley, the man selected for this assignment did not sail direct to Africa, but he went first to India. Finally arriving at Zanzibar he commenced to make arrangements for his difficult journey inland. Two months later he was on his way in search of Livingstone "dead or alive," as his editor had told him.

Stanley, like David, needed a large number of porters. He was transporting food and medical supplies not only for his own journey, but also he carried with him many things that he knew Livingstone would be wanting.

His long file of bearers consisted of one hundred and ninety-two men. Stanley soon came up against some of the difficulties that David had been facing in all his long journeys across Africa. It was heard that David had been in the region of Ujiji. Half way towards this place Stanley fell ill with fever. He was unconscious for two whole weeks. During all this time he kept hearing the voice of his editor repeating, "Find Livingstone! Find Livingstone! Find Livingstone!" This was a time of great strain for Stanley. He had come so far, but who could say whether there was still any trace of Livingstone? He might have been dead a long time, and all his African friends might be dead also, or scattered far from Ujiji.

Despair began to steal over him. It was tempting to say that it was proved that the man for whom he was looking was dead, that there were no signs to bring back to show the people at home. Just at this crucial time something occurred that changed his life. While he was ill, he had plenty of time to think, and his mind wandered back to his early days. When he was a boy, and then later as a young man, he used to go to church and read his Bible, and so in the middle of the jungle, recovering from his illness, he pulled out his Bible. He read the familiar passages and then something happened. God spoke to him, in a way that God speaks to everyone who will stop and listen, and Stanley prayed for forgiveness that he had forgotten God all these years. He had come to Africa searching for David Livingstone, but the first person he found was God.

This did not mean the end of his difficulties. The undergrowth was just as dense, the swamps just as treacherous, but it did mean that Stanley was given the strength to overcome all the troubles he faced. He no longer gave in to the idea that had been buzzing in his head, to quit and go home. He wrote in his diary, "While I can walk I am going on, and I will not leave Africa without Livingstone."

Starting out again on their way to Ujiji, the party came upon a lake. It was terribly hot, and the air was so damp that the handkerchief that Stanley continually wiped across his forehead was wringing wet. The lake looked very cool in the shade of the overhanging trees, and without hesitation Stanley took off his clothes and was just about to dive in when one of the bearers called to him. He froze and then saw something in the water move. Suddenly he realized that the dark object at the lake's edge that he had assumed was a tree root was in fact the snout of a huge crocodile!

Their troubles extended far beyond the dangerous creatures that inhabited the African interior. One day they came upon a battle. Some Arab slave-traders had tried to capture slaves from a tribe who lived in the country through which Stanley had to pass. When Stanley's party arrived the natives were getting the best of it, and the bearers soon joined in on their side, but unfortunately the Arabs came back at them with such force that the natives were scattered and Stanley nearly lost his life. Several of his men were killed, but the rest continued the exhausting march. Sometimes they showed signs of mutiny and Stanley had to pretend that he would turn them over to the slavers, or that he would shoot them as he did the wild beasts that they cooked and ate on the way. This was the only way Stanley found he could keep them together. When they were happy they would sing, but when they were unhappy they threatened to run away, which would certainly have meant the death of Stanley. How differently Stanley and Livingstone treated the men who served them. Stanley's method may have been effective, but his men were never devoted to him the way David's were.

As they came to a village one morning, after marching since dawn, a very excited native rushed up to Stanley and said that there was a white man in the village. The news was staggering. Could Livingstone really be here? If it was not Livingstone, who could it be? But it must be the end of his search—no other white man had ever been as far as this, so surely this must be Livingstone! In a few moments Stanley was shown to the hut from which a pale face looked out; but a brief glance showed that this was not Livingstone, but a native whose skin was paler than the rest—an albino—but not a white man. The great disappointment was hard to bear. At one instant Stanley was full of expectancy, and in the next all his hopes had been crushed. Taking courage he told his porters that the search must go on.

Soon they arrived at another village where some natives sat around resting. They were not local men as even Stanley could see. They belonged to the tribe that had its home much nearer to the coast, and when he asked them what they were doing there, the answer came, "We are taking the supplies for the Doctor." This was the party that had left Zanzibar several months before Stanley, and they appeared to be quite happy to take a long rest half way. Stanley knew what the supplies would mean to Livingstone, and how eagerly he would be looking for his mail, so he told the porters to get on their way and quickly. He took with him the man who had been carrying the precious letters from David's family and friends at home, and left the others to follow behind.

A few days later at Ujiji, David's faithful African boy Susi, ran to him crying, "An Englishman! I see him!" David, a "mere ruckle of bones," with his supplies nearly exhausted and his strength ebbing away, could not believe it, but in a few minutes Stanley came forward, raising his hat. Words came easily to the journalist as a rule, yet when he stood face to face with Livingstone, the man for whom he had been searching nearly a whole year, tears came to his eyes and all he could say was, "Doctor Livingstone, I presume!"—A phrase with which he might have greeted anyone in his office back home in New York.

The two men shook hands. "I thank God, Doctor, I have been permitted to see you," said Stanley.

"I feel thankful," replied David Livingstone, "that I am here to welcome you." This was on October 28, 1871. Stanley was just in time. He brought David new life. For long months Livingstone had not seen a white man or heard a word spoken in the English language. There were so many questions that David wished to ask. So much had been happening in the outside world about which he had heard nothing. There was no radio network with news broadcasts to keep him in touch with what was going on. There was no telegraph service, no telephone, no faster way of reaching him than the way Stanley had come. Stanley brought David the letters from his children and news of his family as well as tidings of the outside world, strange and thrilling for the lonely exile. They stayed together until March 14, 1872—over four months.

During this time Stanley watched with the eye of a newspaperman the way in which Livingstone went about his work. He was one of only a very few who were able to watch him caring for the Africans, giving them medicine, advice, all sorts of help in various ways, beside doing his most important work, preaching the Gospel of his Master. Stanley went on to write the *Autobiography of Henry M. Stanley*, which records his experiences in finding David and his impressions of that great man.

On the morning after his arrival at Livingstone's camp, Stanley woke up with a start. He thought he could hear a choir singing, and he rubbed his eyes and pinched himself to make sure that he was not still asleep. He was most certainly wide awake, but where did the sound of those fine deep voices come from? He had rarely heard such a wonderful chorus back home, but to hear a choir in the heart of Africa was the last thing that Stanley had expected. Now he recognized the music. It was a hymn he used to sing very often, and now it was being sung with a great deal of gusto: "Onward Christian Soldiers!" came the chorus, and before he knew it, Stanley found himself joining in. All of a sudden it stopped. Livingstone came into the hut and apologized for waking Stanley so early.

"It was our usual choir practice," he said. "I hope you were not disturbed by it."

Every day after that Stanley was up in time to take part in the choir practice too, and while David swung his arms about with terrific enthusiasm keeping them in time, Stanley added his tenor to the lusty bass and resounding treble voices of the Africans.

In celebration of Stanley's arrival, David and the people of Ujiji had a great feast. The boys of the village were told to chase after the fatted pig, and a scramble began with the squealing pig evading them all the time until cornered against the wall of a hut. Then the cook took charge and started to prepare the evening meal.

Meanwhile Stanley tried to answer the countless questions David put to him. The letters from home had told him a lot of personal news that he was glad to have, but he had been for months with no newspaper, and a great many important events had been happening of which he was entirely ignorant. The two men talked at great length, and their discussion covered a very wide range of subjects.

At last the time came for the feast, and though he was not in the habit of eating much, Livingstone joined in the fun and enjoyed the welcome party in honor of his unexpected guest. The company of another white man was a real tonic to Livingstone, as he wrote in his diary, and after his arrival they both had four meals a day in contrast to the two a day previously, and David's health improved as a result.

It was soon a very healthy Livingstone who was able to set out on a voyage of exploration around the northern part of Lake Tanganyika.

Once more they needed many porters to carry the food, medicines, beads (which would buy them anything they wanted from the local people through whose country they might pass) and other necessaries such as rifles to shoot lions or elephants if they should attack their party. It was always wise to be ready for that kind of an adventure! This time there were also the sextant, compass and chronometer that David needed in his making of maps of this unknown part of the continent.

Each day readings would be taken and David would write them down carefully in his notebook, then as he was able, he made these readings into a map. This kind of map is known as a "contour" map because it traces the "contours" or places that are at an equal height above sea level. David was at this time trying to establish where the source of the Nile river lay, and he thought it was near Lake Tanganyika. In later years, this assumption was proven incorrect, but his accurate and carefully noted observations were still extremely valuable. From his maps, the true structure of the hills of the region was first learned.

Stanley now began to think about the journey home, and asked Livingstone when he would be ready to start out. The surprising reply came quickly, "I cannot leave Africa with my work unfinished."

"But surely, my dear doctor, you don't seriously think of staying here now that I have found you?" Stanley asked.

"I was not lost," David replied. "Nor was I hiding." He was surprised to learn that Stanley had supposed he would now return to England.

This announcement of David's resolve to stay did not please Stanley very much. His editor, he knew, hoped that there would be an opportunity for an exclusive story from the pen of Livingstone, but that was not to be. The newspaper reporter would have to undertake that lengthy trek homeward on his own just as he had come.

Stanley could see that Livingstone would not leave Africa while there was strength in his body, and after he became feeble from the renewed attacks of fever which were sure to come, he would die on the continent for which he had worked so hard and so long. Although he realized that it was useless, Stanley argued with David and tried to persuade him to come home.

"You're front page news, you know, Doctor!" he told him. "There would be lecture tours and articles for you to write to arouse interest in the work out here."

David was not a little surprised to hear that he was "front page news." This provided a contrast to the situation as he saw it while waiting for months on end in the heart of the jungle for badly needed supplies. There had been time when he was refused things that were absolutely essential for his work, and the difficulties caused in such a way gave him much discouragement.

There arrived one day at David's hut a strong native with a thorn in his foot. The thorn had gone in very deep and the wound had turned septic. It proved necessary to use a knife to extract it properly. In those days there was no ether or morphine to ease the patient's suffering, so Stanley had a part to play in this operation. As David prepared the wound, Stanley took hold of the patient's arms to prevent him from struggling. In a few moments the doctor removed the troublesome thorn and the grateful native went away with a bandage on his foot. It was a frequent occurrence for the natives to be bothered by thorns in this way because they didn't wear shoes, and until the arrival of the doctor this often meant a great deal of pain. Sometimes the wound might have even been the cause of death.

David was not only concerned with healing the disease that he found about him, but also he was anxious to show the natives how Jesus cared for them. They came to David with their various troubles, whatever they might be, for they always found him ready to help them, and he always seemed to know the best way out of any difficult situation.

All this Stanley watched with great interest. He later wrote that one could take any point in Livingstone's character and analyze it carefully, and that he would challenge any man to find a fault in it. "His gentleness never forsook him," said Stanley, "and his hopefulness never deserted him. No harassing anxieties, distraction of mind, long separation from home and kindred could make him complain. He thought all would come out right at last, he had such faith in the goodness of providence. To the stern dictates of duty he sacrificed home and ease, the pleasures, refinements and luxuries of civilized life. His was the Spartan heroism, the inflexibility of the Roman, the enduring resolution of the Anglo-Saxon never to relinquish his work though his heart yearned for home, never to surrender his obligations till he could write 'Finis' to his work. "In him," wrote Stanley, "religion exhibited its loveliest features; it governed his conduct, not only towards his servants, but towards the natives, the Mohammedans, and all who came in contact with him. Without religion, Livingstone, with his ardent temperament, his enthusiasm, his high spirit and courage, must have become uncompanionable and a hard master. Religion tamed him and made him a Christian gentleman; the crude and willful have been refined and subdued; religion has made him the most companionable of men and indulgent of masters, a man whose society is pleasurable to a degree."

Now Stanley was to make ready for his return journey. Among the letters which he had brought for the doctor was one from his daughter in which she told her father that though she would very much like to see him she would be much happier to know that he was staying if he thought that was right. His daughter's display of real spirit was a tremendous encouragement to Livingstone.

The day for the party to leave came at last and the doctor arranged to accompany them part of the way to Zanzibar and then to leave Stanley to go on alone.

As the bearers strode along under the loads, the tall grasses almost hid the front of the column from David's view. Suddenly the men stopped dead in their tracks. Livingstone and Stanley went up to the front to see what was happening and they were faced by a ferocious band of tribesmen. The savage-looking men carried long blow pipes through which they shot poisoned arrows with deadly aim. Livingstone wasted no time. In just a few short minutes, these dangerous people could wipe out their entire party. Summoning the courage God had blessed him with, he boldly walked up to them and told them that he was a white man who had never harmed a black man and that he loved the people of Africa. Without an argument or a threat or a single arrow fired, the natives disappeared back into the long grass. David's bravery deeply impressed Stanley. The ordeal was over almost before it had begun, and Livingstone was calmly leading his party on again.

After a few days march from Ujiji, Stanley told Livingstone with much regret that he thought that it was time for him to turn back.

The parting of these two men was full of good wishes that each might have a safe journey, Stanley to the coast to send back supplies to David and David himself back into the heart of the continent to make maps and to open up the interior of Africa. Stanley perhaps knew in his heart that he would be the last white man to see David and it was all the more difficult to say goodbye and leave him there so alone.

Livingstone told him, "You have done what few men could do—far better than some great travelers I know—and

I am grateful to you for what you have done for me. God guide you safe home and bless you, my friend. Farewell!"

When Stanley left he still had many weary miles of swamp, jungle and disease-ridden country to cover. There were still hostile natives through whose country he must pass, and it was some months later that he arrived at Zanzibar. He arranged for the supplies to be sent to David, choosing men as his experience had taught him. He had begun to know the right sort of man to employ, for some of those whom he had chosen previously had not been much help; they had run off in ones and twos with what they had on their heads, or they had been quarrelsome. He sent his party on their way, and then set out for England with the news of Livingstone.

Once Stanley reached England, however, some people thought he was not telling the truth, and it was heartbreaking after all the difficulties that he had encountered that he should have to face such accusations of being a fraud. It was not possible to convince some of his critics that he was indeed speaking the truth until further news came from Africa to say that Livingstone's body had been brought to the coast by some of his African servants.

After Stanley went on his way to Zanzibar, David had gone back to Ujiji to await the supplies that he promised to send. He had a long time to wait, six long months altogether, and this was a long time for David to be kept in one place. As soon as the supplies came through he set off again on a further exploration. But this was to be his last, for after so many years in the heat and swamp, the endurance of David's body had finally reached its limit. He became steadily weaker until he couldn't walk. He rode a donkey for a while, but his strength failed for even that and at last he was carried in a litter, a sort of hammock tied onto a bamboo pole carried by two natives. They could not help swinging it to and fro as they went along, and so this was not quite so luxurious a form of travel as might be thought. By this time David was sixty years of age. Livingstone's life had been a terribly hard one—he had traveled 29,000 miles in Africa. Now he was "knocked up quite," as he wrote in his diary. He still had the heart of a lion, and giving up did not enter into his thoughts. But on April 29, thirteen months after saying goodbye to Stanley, he was carried into a village called Ilala, where his faithful bearers built a hut to shelter him from the rain. They laid him inside, and Susi kept watch at the door. Two mornings later Susi, looking inside, saw David on his knees as if he were praying. As he did not move, Susi went in to him; but David Livingstone was dead. Death had touched him gently as he prayed, and he had passed into a happier world to be with Jesus, whom he had loved and served so well.

CHAPTER 10

To the Coast

David's faithful servants, Susi and Chuma, showed their love for him in the best way they knew how. They first buried his heart under a tree. His "heart" had always been in Africa, and they felt that it always should be. There are many monuments in different places in commemoration of Livingstone, but none can be quite as meaningful as the place where that tree stood. Indeed, perhaps it is still there today.

When they had roughly embalmed David's body, they wrapped it very carefully in a cloth, and tied their precious load to a bamboo pole, as they had done his hammock when he was too ill to walk, and a small band of them set off for the coast. It was a distance of 1,500 miles and the intrepid party began with a prayer, as well as a great deal of faith and devotion, in their hearts.

They had been on their way only a little while when the trouble began. The swamps through which they had to pass were always inclined to give them fever, for the tetse flies are more numerous and therefore more effective over swampy country. Fever struck them again and again, as well as a more serious complaint. A form of rheumatism, usually only found in older people, pained their bodies. With so many miles to cover, they could not hope to get very far if their speed was greatly reduced by such illnesses, but far from getting depressed and giving up, they struggled on until they came to higher ground.

Even having crossed the swamp, their difficulties were not ended. They still had to cross the Luapula. This river was four miles wide at the point at which they had to cross it, four miles up to their waists in the strong current in which crocodiles were always to be found. Happily, there were no hungry crocodiles on that particular day and the party crossed in safety.

They enjoyed a brief rest when they reached the other side and dried in the hot sun. As they set out again, they felt hostile eyes watching them. It did not take them long to discover that the local inhabitants were not pleased to see them, and a spear narrowly missed the first man in the column, warning them not to go any further. But these devoted servants of David had not come so far just to be scared away with a few spears and arrows, and they continued steadily on. The way was immediately barred

by a ferocious band of warriors who demanded to know
who it was that they were carrying in the cloth. It seemed
that the news of their journey had gone before them, and
the faithful band had to pretend to turn back or they would
have all been killed. They decided that it would be quite
impossible to travel through this particular territory with
the body so obviously visible. A little scheme was planned.
A reel of cloth was done up in imitation of the one in which
Livingstone's body was being carried, and a few of them
then went on in a direct route with this bundle. When the
hostile natives saw that it was only cloth that they were
carrying they were allowed to pass. Meanwhile the rest
of the small band carried the actual body by a devious
route that avoided the villages. Expert in the knowledge
of the forest and how to move about it without making
any noise, they rejoined the decoy party later on when
they were well clear of the interfering natives. The reason
why the local people did not want the body of Livingstone
to be brought across their land was their fear that it
would bring them bad luck. The tribal witch doctors were
extremely influential and when they declared something
good or bad, it was very difficult indeed to convince the
tribe that there was no truth in what they had been told.
David had spent a great deal of time trying to overcome
the deeply entrenched tribal superstitions. Sometimes it
was extremely difficult, but other times, given the right
circumstances, it could be done quickly. For instance

the case when he used a burning glass to make the grass catch fire; this at once gained for him the confidence of the natives who, a moment before, had wanted to spear him to death because their witch doctor had told them that he brought bad luck.

A little further on Susi, Chuma and the rest of their party came into more hostile territory. These tribes did not mind what they were carrying, they simply attacked them on sight and the small and weary band had to fight back as best they could. It was certainly a one-sided battle, but they were equipped with rifles, and this did more than anything else to frighten the attackers away.

One day they came upon a party of white men. The Royal Geographical Society—the society for which David had been doing some of his exploration—had sent these men out. The white men, knowing something of the difficulties of travel under any circumstances through the forests and swamps, were amazed at the courage of this band of Africans who had already come hundreds of miles on their way to the coast with the body of Livingstone. It was proposed to them that they should bury the body there where the two parties had met, but the Africans would not hear of it. They had so far been given the strength to carry on, and their determination was no less than when they had started out.

There were still more natives who had heard about the party bringing the body of Livingstone to the coast.

They wanted to make them pay in cloth, in "valuables" such as mirrors and beads, and in anything that the small party had with them, for the privilege of carrying the body through their country. They were caused much delay on account of this, and so another scheme was thought of to make the journey easier. It was spread abroad that Livingstone had been buried and the body was again wrapped in cloth to disguise it from curious eyes, and since news travels fast in Africa through the beat of the tom-tom, it was soon proclaimed throughout the country lying between them and the coast that the body of Livingstone was no longer on its way, but had been buried. This scheme was very helpful since nobody doubted that it was just a bale of cloth that they were now carrying.

The brave men were on the last stage of the journey when a large snake appeared suddenly from the dense undergrowth. It raced straight to a little girl who was walking with them carrying a water pot. The deadly sting struck her like a sharp knife and in a few moments she collapsed. She was tenderly picked up and carried, but after a few steps, the snake's poison accomplished its work and she died. Not long after, a party of Arabs passed the same place, and one of their number was struck down as well. They hardly had time to notice what was wrong with the one who had been stung before he too fell down dead. They saw the little grave in which the girl had been laid and buried the Arab man beside her.

Finally the party bearing Livingstone's body reached Bagamoio on the coast. Here they gave the body over to the charge of the representatives of the British government. There was not much fuss made about it, and nobody there seemed to have thought of the immense effort that went into the transporting of David's body all that way. One man, however, did realize something of what they had done, and paid for three of the faithful natives to go to London to pay their last respects to their beloved leader.

Epilogue

Brought by a liner back home to England the body of Livingstone was laid to rest in Westminster Abbey during a great funeral service, at which the three African followers were present. A black marble stone marks the place where he was buried. On it are these words, which commemorate also the heroic journey undertaken by the faithful natives:

BROUGHT BY FAITHFUL HANDS

OVER LAND AND SEA,

HERE RESTS

DAVID LIVINGSTONE

MISSIONARY,

TRAVELLER,

PHILANTHROPIST,

BORN MARCH 19TH, 1813

AT BLANTYRE, LANARKSHIRE,

DIED MAY 4TH, 1873

AT CHETAMBO'S VILLAGE, ULALA.

Along the right border of the stone are the words:

> TANTUS AMOR VERI, NIHIL
> EST QUOD NOSCERE MALIM,
> QUAM FLUVII CAUSAS PER
> SAECULA TANTA LATENTES.

And along the left border:

> OTHER SHEEP HAVE I WHICH
> ARE NOT OF THIS FOLD; THEM
> ALSO MUST I BRING, AND
> THEY SHALL HEAR MY VOICE.

For thirty years his life was spent in an unwearied effort to evangelize the native races, to explore the undiscovered secrets, and to abolish the desolating slave trade of Central Africa, where with his last words he wrote:

> "All I can say in my solitude is, may Heaven's rich blessing come down on everyone—American, English or Turk—who will help to heal this open sore of the world."

A few of the things David Livingstone was known for saying are worth remembering:

"Fear God and work hard."

"I can be rich without money."

"A life of selfishness is one of misery."

"Be manly Christians and never do a mean thing."

"Depend upon it, a kind word or deed is never lost."

"I shall not swerve a hairbreadth from my work while life is spared."

"Science and Religion are not hostile but friendly to each other."

"One of the discoveries I have made is that there are vast numbers of good people in the world."

"I view the end of the geographical feat as the beginning of the missionary enterprise."

"Nothing earthly will make me give up my work in despair. I encourage myself in the Lord my God, and go forward."

"Good works gain the approbation of the world, and though there is antipathy in the human heart to the Gospel of Christ, yet when Christians make their good work shine, all admire them."

Livingstone tried to open Africa to the Gospel and commerce, to end the slave trade, and to solve big problems in geography and science. And at every stage in his efforts he got rebuffs. First the Missionary Society directors did not quite share his idea that before Central Africa could be evangelized it must be explored, and that he was the man to explore it. Then some of the white missionaries were jealous of him, and made his task harder, though they saw their mistake later and were proud of their great leader. Then Mrs. Livingstone died and left her husband lonely, and with his little motherless children far away. Wherever he went in Africa he found horrors and tragedies that he vainly tried to cure. When the British Government entrusted him with an exploring mission, it had not patience to see it through, and stopped sending money to pay the cost. Troubles met him at every turn. Delays upset his plans. Worries pressed upon him. He suffered thirst and hunger. Fever and dysentery laid him low. Always he ran the risk of being killed by hostile natives or by sly slave-dealers. His stores got lost or stolen. His papers sank in a wrecked ship. His journeys through dense forests and over trackless deserts wore him down. His supplies of clothing ran short. Time and time again he just escaped death by accidents to canoes. Wild beasts threatened him. Guides failed him. Savage chiefs denied him passage through their country. He went months at a time without a letter from home, or a glimpse of a white face. Yet he bore all this, and even his journals reveal that while now and again he was downhearted, he was generally cheerful and always brave. He lived very close to his God and his Bible was his greatest solace. He felt daily the companionship of Jesus Christ even when he was most solitary.

At just five feet six inches tall with a slender build, it was not bodily strength, but power of will, that carried David along, and made him able to trudge along, day after day, with that "forward tread, firm, simple, resolute, neither fast nor slow, no hurry and no dawdle."

Livingstone lived his life and did his work fired by a great ideal. He believed that God Himself had called him to open Africa; and having opened it he left it to others, under God's guidance, to take up the task where he laid it down.

David Livingstone passed from this life many many years ago; but his name is honored and his fame is ever fresh, because he lived nobly and died nobly, and because he led a great crusade in a way which made other brave men come forward to see that it was carried on. There are a lot of missionaries who are working in the Mission Field because of David Livingstone. Africa is dotted all over with Mission stations, and, just as David believed, the Gospel of Jesus Christ fast destroyed the slave trade. While others had awakened the minds and consciences of people at home to this great evil, he did more perhaps than any man to end this dreadful traffic, which was still being carried on despite the fact that it was against the law. So many slaves owe their freedom and so many men owe their lives to Dr. Livingstone, whose deathless story I have tried to tell that you may love him; but most of all so that you may love the same Lord Jesus who made David Livingstone the hero that he was.

CHRONOLOGY OF EVENTS IN LIVINGSTONE'S LIFE

1813 Born at Blantyre, in Lanarkshire, Scotland, March 19.

1833 Real conversion took place in his life.

1836 Entered school in Glasgow.

1838 Accepted by London Missionary Society, September.

1840 Ordained missionary in Albion St. Chapel, November 20.
      Sailed on H.M. Ship "George" for Africa, December 8.

1841 Arrived at Kuruman, July 31.

1842 Extended tour of Bechuana country begun February 10.

1843 Located at Mabotsa, August.

1844 Marriage to Mary Moffat of Kuruman.

1846 Located at Chonuane with Chief Sechele.

1847 Moved to Kolobeng.

1848 Sechele, first convert, baptized, October 1.

1849   Lake 'Ngami discovered, August 1.

1850   Royal Geographical Society awarded royal donation, 25 guineas.

1851   Discovered the upper Zambesi August 3.

1852   Mrs. Livingstone and four children sailed from Cape Town April 23.

1853   Journey from Linyanti to west coast, November 11 to May 31, 1854.

1854   French Geographical Society awarded silver medal;

        University of Glasgow conferred degree LL.D.;

        Journey from west coast back to Linyanti, September 24 to September 11, 1855.

1855   Journey from Linyanti to Quilimane on east coast, November 3 to May 20, 1856;
        Royal Geographical Society awarded Patron's Gold Medal.

1856   Arrived in London on first visit home, December 9.

1857   Freedom of cities of London, Glasgow, Edinburgh, Dundee and many other towns; Corresponding Member of American Geographical and Statistical Society, New York; Royal Geographical Society, London; Geographical Society of Paris; K.K. Geographical Society of Vienna; Honorary Fellow of

Faculty and Physicians of Glasgow; Degree of D.C.L. by University of Oxford; elected F.H.S.; appointed Commander of Zambcsi Expedition and her Majesty's Consul at Tette, Quilimane, Senna

1858   Returned with Mrs. Livingstone to Africa, March 10.

1859   River Shire explored and Lake Nyassa discovered, September 16.

1862   Mrs. Livingstone died at Shupanga, April 27;

Explored the Yovuma River.

1864   Arrived in Bombay, June 13; London, July 23.

1866   Arrived at Zanzibar, January 28.

1867   Discovered Lake Tanganyika April.

1868   Discovered Lake Bangweolo, July 18.

1869   Arrived at Ujiji, March 14.

1871   Reached Nyangwe, March 29; returned to Ujiji a "living skeleton," October 23.
Henry M. Stanley found him October 28.

1872   Gold Medal by Italian Geographical Society.

1873   Died in his tent at Ilala, May 1.

1874   Body buried with honors in Westminster Abbey, London, April 18.

Lessons from Livingstone's life:

YOUR OBSERVATIONS

_____

_____

_____

_____

_____

_____

_____

_____

_____

_____

_____

_____

_____

_____

_____

_____

_____

_____

_____

_____

_____

_____

_____

_____

_____

_____

_____

_____

_____

_____

_____

_____

_____

_____

_____

_____

_____

_____

_____

_____

_____

_____

_____

_____

_____

_____

_____

_____

_____

_____

_____

_____

_____

_____

_____

_____

_____

_____

_____

_____

_____

_____

_____

_____

_____

_____

_____

_____

_____

_____

_____

_____

ROBERT MORRISON
Translator in China

Robert Morrison was the first Protestant missionary to China and a forerunner of the modern medical missionaries. He accomplished incredible things for God, including a translation of the Bible into Chinese, an Anglo-Chinese dictionary, and hundreds of Chinese tracts and translations.

Morrison toiled for twenty-five years in China, and though his ministry was not blessed by great numbers of converts, he paved the way for other missionaries to come to China. His work for Christ was what mattered, not the praise of friends or the blame of his enemies. He worked ceaselessly, never faltering from the path of duty, which enabled him to accomplish work which seemed impossible. To all Christians he is a wonderful example.

ISBN 1-932307-26-5, $5.99/£4.99 (ages 8-13)

The Great "By Faith" Biography Series

MARY SLESSOR
Faith in West Africa

Perhaps the greatest thing that can be said of Mary Slessor is that she was a born missionary. From her earliest days, her dream was to be a missionary and Calabar (Nigeria) was her mission field. The death of David Livingstone was the catalyst for her missionary call, and in 1876, she went to the African mission field.

"Anywhere, provided it be forward," was one of her most famous sayings and summed up her life. She toiled for forty years in the heart of Nigeria, constantly seeking new tribes and new people to reach with the gospel of Christ. She rescued hundreds of orphans from certain death, prevented wars between tribes, helped to heal the sick, and spoke ceaselessly of the great love of God in sending Jesus Christ.

ISBN 1-932307-25-7, $6.99/£5.99 (ages 14-19)

The Great "By Faith" Biography Series

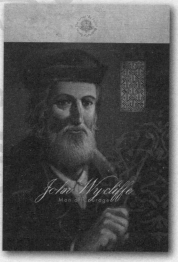

JOHN WYCLIFFE
Man of Courage

John Wycliffe, the Morning Star of the Reformation, gave us the first English translation of the Bible. A noted scholar and teacher at Oxford, his reliance on the Bible as the sole source of truth stood in stark contrast to the teachings of the Catholic church. His followers went out, teaching and preaching to the common man throughout England.

Bowing himself to the authority of the Bible, his great aim was to bring men to the Word. He saw it as the one great authority, the Law that exceeded all other laws. His life's work continued through men like John Hus and laid the groundwork for Martin Luther, John Calvin, John Knox and the other great men of the Reformation.

ISBN 1-932307-27-3, $5.99/£4.99 (ages 14-19)

The Great "By Faith" Biography Series